Bridges

Contents

Bridges   2

Bridges of the World   6

The Bridge Is Down!   16

Harry and Larry Build a Bridge   24

Bridges

Written by Ashley King

Bridges carry people over water.
They carry people
over valleys and roads.
Some bridges carry trains.
Some carry cars and trucks.

How do bridges carry
these heavy things?
Bridges are very strong.

Some are made of stone.
Some are made of wood.
Some are made of steel.
Some are made of concrete.

Many bridges have arches.
Arches make a bridge strong.

Many bridges have steel cables.
The cables help hold up
the bridge.

Some bridges can open.
When the bridge is up,
big boats can go under it.

Bridges of

Written by Janne Galbraith

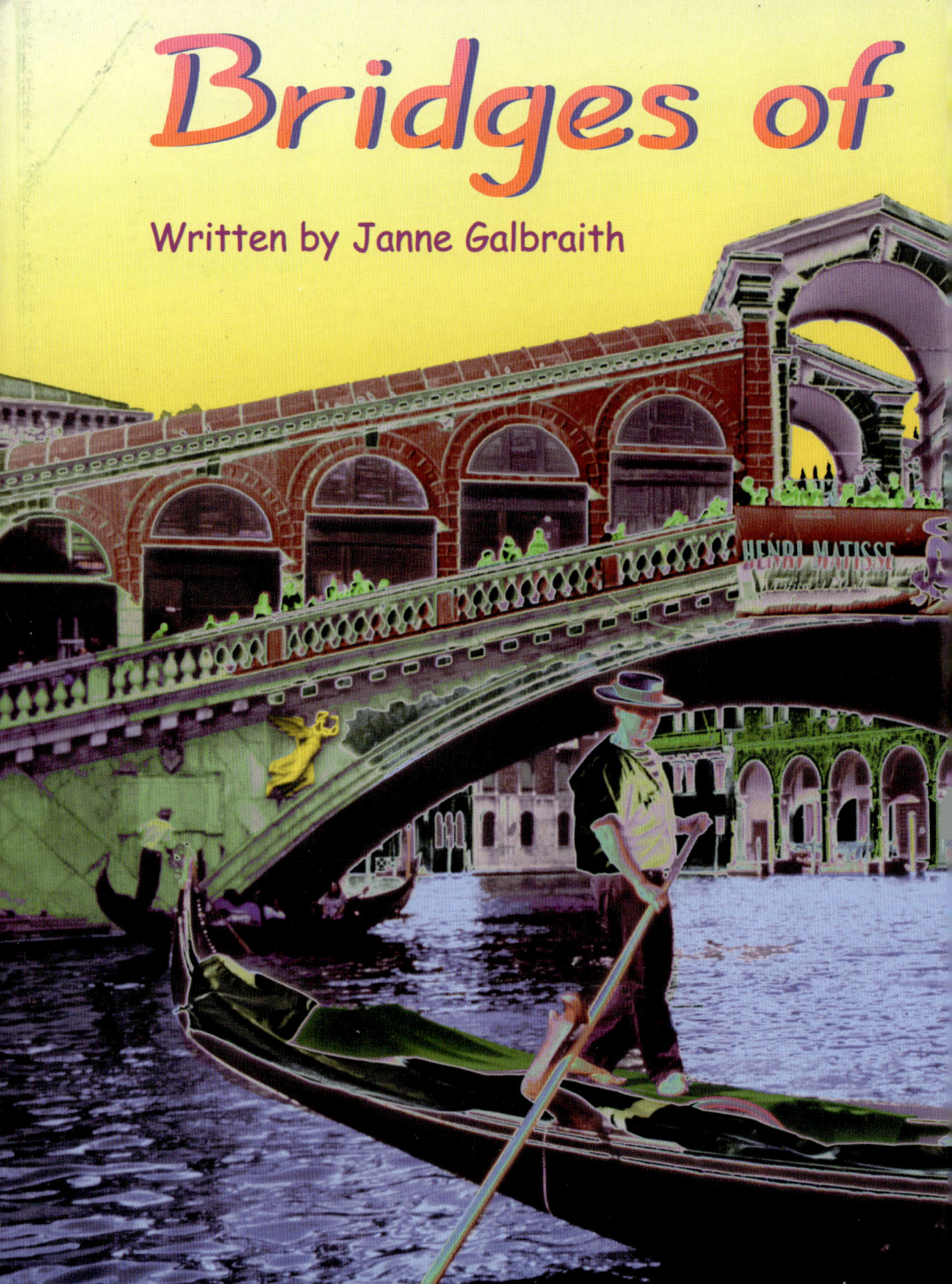

6 **Place:** Venice, Italy   **Across:** The Grand Canal   **Built:** 1591

the World

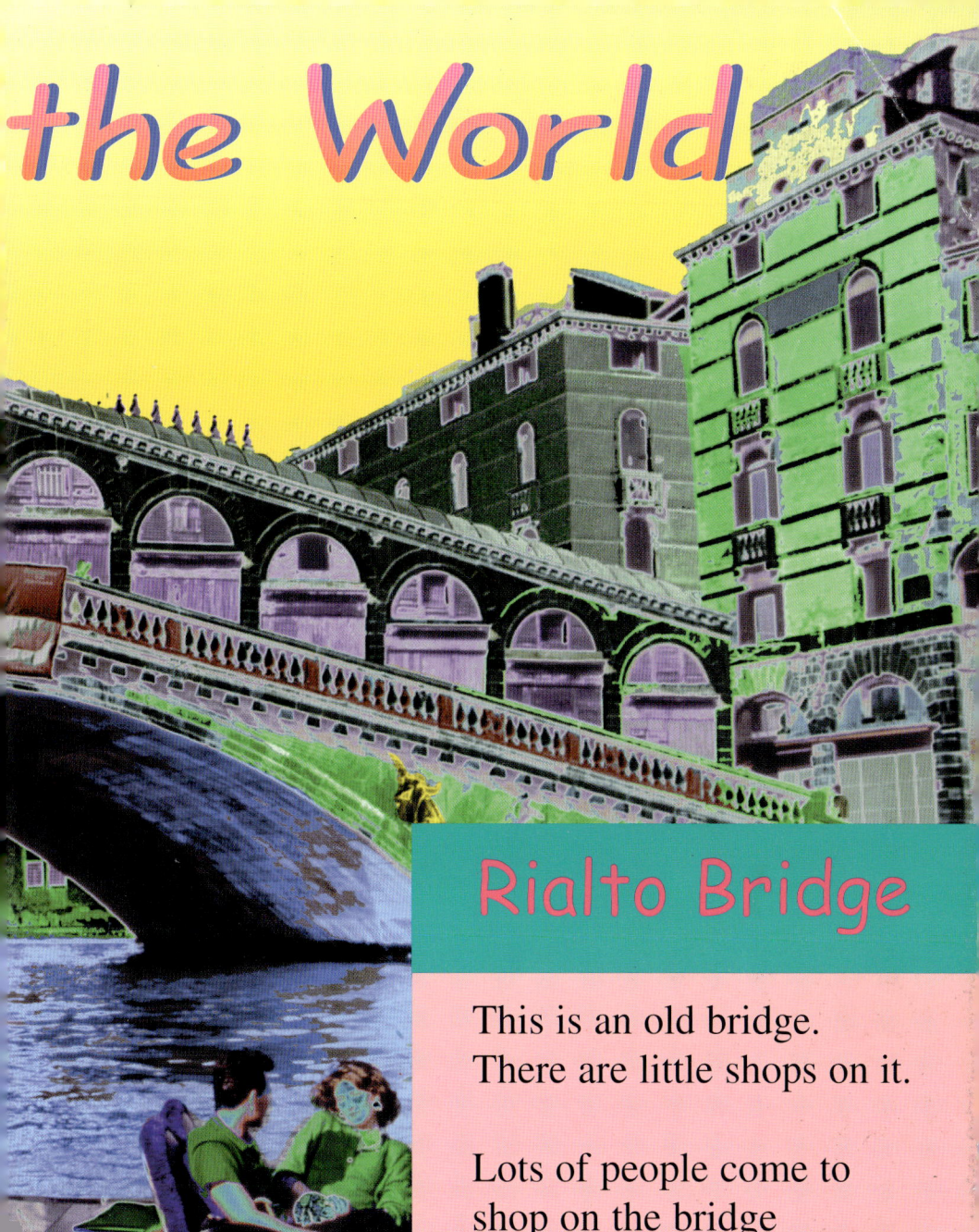

Rialto Bridge

This is an old bridge.
There are little shops on it.

Lots of people come to
shop on the bridge
and to ride boats under it.

Length: 89 feet (27 m)   **Materials:** Marble   **Type:** Arch

Built: 1883   **Length:** 1,595 feet (486 m)

Bridge

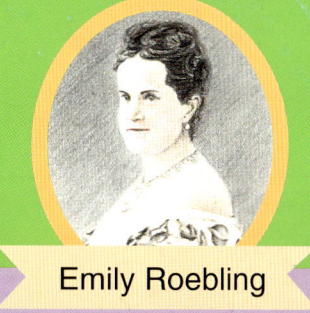
Emily Roebling

A man named Washington Roebling
was in charge of building
the Brooklyn Bridge.
Washington went underwater every day
to make sure that the towers were well built.
But, one day, he got the bends.

Washington could not walk or see very well.
He could not even write.
So every day, his wife, Emily,
went to the Brooklyn Bridge for him.
Emily worked very hard
to make sure the bridge was well built.

When the Brooklyn Bridge was finished,
the people of New York had a party.
Everyone thanked
the Roeblings for their help.
Emily was the first person
to ride over the Brooklyn Bridge.

Tower Bridge

This is the Tower Bridge.
It has two big towers
that look like castles.

The Tower Bridge
can open up
so boats can go under it.
Cars go across the bridge
when it is down.
People can walk over
the Tower Bridge, too.

Place: London, England   **Across:** Thames River   **Built:** 1894

Skippers Canyon Bridge

Lots of people come to this bridge.
But they do not come
just to walk over it.
They come to jump off it!
People like to bungee jump
off this bridge.
They tie a bungee rope
to their legs.
When they jump off the bridge,
the bungee rope
keeps them from hitting the ground.
The people bounce up and down
in the air.
Then they are helped
to the ground.

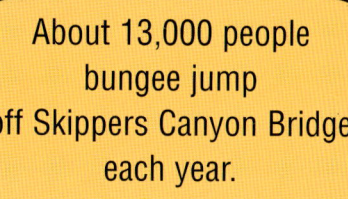

About 13,000 people
bungee jump
off Skippers Canyon Bridge
each year.

Place: New Zealand   **Across:** Skippers Canyon   **Built:** 1898

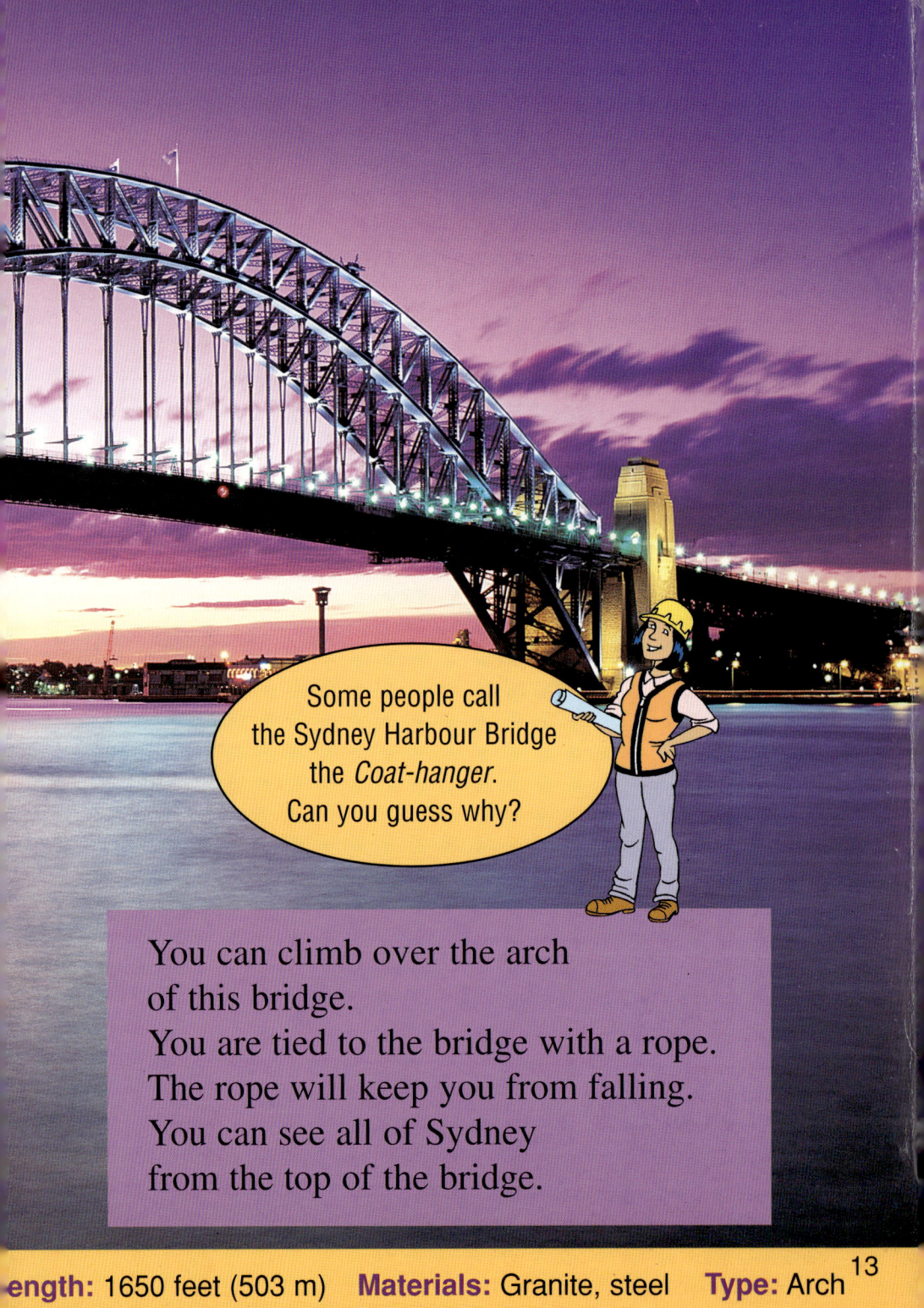

Some people call the Sydney Harbour Bridge the *Coat-hanger*. Can you guess why?

You can climb over the arch of this bridge.
You are tied to the bridge with a rope.
The rope will keep you from falling.
You can see all of Sydney from the top of the bridge.

ength: 1650 feet (503 m)　**Materials:** Granite, steel　**Type:** Arch

Sydney Harbour Bridge

This is the widest bridge in the world. Cars and trains go over it.

Place: Sydney, Australia   **Across:** Sydney Harbour   **Built:** 1932

Length: 200 feet (61 m)   Materials: Bricks, steel   Type: Bascule

Place: New York, USA   **Across:** East River

Brooklyn

Washington Roebling

The Brooklyn Bridge is in New York.
It goes from Brooklyn to Manhattan.

The Brooklyn Bridge crosses a deep river.
It has two high towers
that begin under the water.
The towers help make the bridge strong.

Building the towers under the water
was very hard.
Some of the people
who worked underwater got very sick.
They got a sickness called *the bends*.

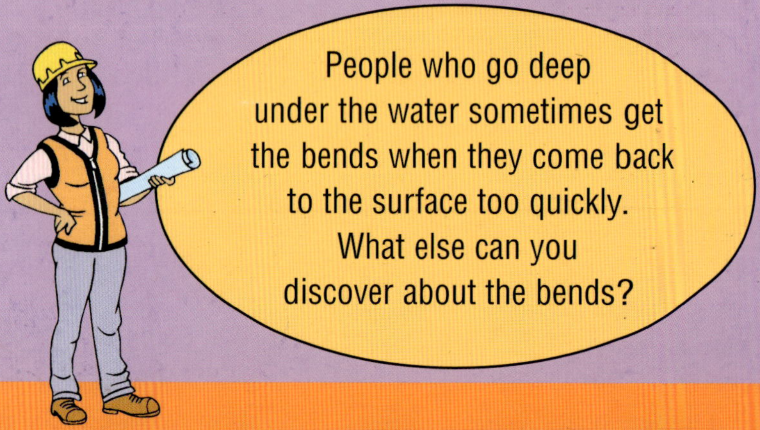

People who go deep under the water sometimes get the bends when they come back to the surface too quickly. What else can you discover about the bends?

Length: 305 feet (93 m)   **Materials:** Steel, wood   **Type:** Suspension

The Bridge

Written by Janne Galbraith
Illustrated by Marjorie Scott

Mum, Dad, my little brother, Jack, and I were on the train.

We were very happy.
We were going on holiday.

Is Down!

The train was on a bridge
when I heard a bang!
The train had stopped.
I looked out.
Some of the bridge was gone.

Then the lights went out
and there was a bigger bang.
The train fell into the water.

Water came into the train.
I had to get out.
I saw a hand.
I took the hand
and it pulled me
out of the train.

Who might be trying to help the people in the water?

I saw a line of people in the water.
They helped me get out.

I was scared.
Where was I?
Where were my mum and my dad?
Where was my little brother?
Were they safe?

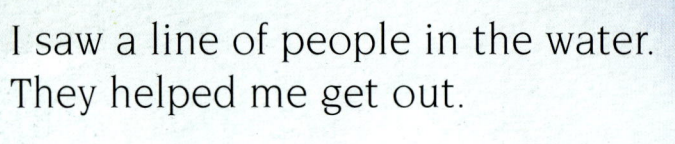

What would you do in a train disaster?
Would you help people get out of the train?

I looked around.
I saw my mum and my dad.
I saw my little brother.
I was so happy.
We were all safe!

The Daily News

Train Disaster! Bridge Gone!

A big wave knocked out the bridge at Tangiwai (*Tung EE why*). The wave washed away the piers that held up the bridge. When the train went onto the bridge, it fell into the river. The wave came from a lake on a volcano not far from the bridge.

"I said stay with me. I said look out for danger!"

"The crane driver did not see you. You did not put on your safety gear."

Later on . . .

This is a pile driver. It puts big poles into the ground. The poles are called piles. They help the bridge stay up.

We make a top for the piles.

We put the bridge together.

We make a road to go over the bridge.

"And we put things on the bridge to help make it safe."

"The bridge is ready! We can go to the beach!"

Index

bends, the	8–9	parts of a bridge	
bridge building	8–9, 24–31	arches	4
building materials	2, 7, 9, 11, 13, 15	cables	4
		piers	22
work site safety	24–27	piles	28
Brooklyn Bridge	8–9	road	30
bungee jumping	14	towers	8, 10
kinds of bridges	2–5	Rialto Bridge	6–7
arch bridges	7, 13	Roebling, Emily	9
bascule bridge	11	Roebling, Washington	8–9
suspension bridge	9, 15		
		Skippers Canyon Bridge	14–15
		Sydney Harbour Bridge	12–13
		Tangiwai Bridge disaster	22–23
		Tower Bridge	10–11